To those who taught me
how to walk through the desert spaces
Exploring with words
Wandering thoughts
Bravely cutting through the thickets
even when there was no
assurance of peaceful shelter

Thank you

I may have gotten a little
sunburnt along the way
but without you
prodding me to
explore the wilderness
I would never have glimpsed
the promised land
and might have remained
forever

In Captivity

The poems in this book
are not all written from my own personal experiences

But they are inspired by the lives
of so many people I have listened to
telling their stories
of pain
heartache
trauma
and toxic Christianity

If you have experienced spiritual abuse
some of these poems might be triggering
Please move slowly through these pages
and tread carefully

Though this book begins in captivity it does not end there
My hope is that you will also find some healing through these words
like I have
and that knowing you are not alone
will bring solace and comfort to your soul

Alternately
my prayer is that we can create a healthier faith community
that does a better job of spreading love and compassion
One that can be trusted to come alongside those
who are struggling to make it through the many

Rocky Patches of Life

Contents

Poet in the Wilderness

Rachel Freeman

Captivity

I want to sing like David
Psalms joyous
heart full of praise

And I do sing
as David crooned
My cries cascade
wailing echoes
in the cavernous void
A landslide of lament

How can I stay
hidden away
cowering as David did
from his enemies
when You have filled
these lungs with breath
that sings a symphony of curses
arias of anger
rhythms of regret

Because I have seen
what has become of Your people
Falling in step
conducted by
Philistines
Egyptians
Pharisees

But it seems
Peter
has used his
sword of letters
to sever the ears
right off their heads

They can no longer hear
my mournful melody

Selah

Hang Paul
over your altars then

If the thorn in his flesh
means more
than the nails in the cross

If his epistles
are more gospel
than the gospels

If his letters hold
more weight than

The Red Letters

Your disappointment
whispers to me
A rumour of my wrongs
going in one ear
and I try to shake it
out the other

But it sticks
in my head
a little ear worm
of my unworthiness

And I wish there was
a love song
I could recall to
replace the derogatory
droning of your voice

Though there is a reason
you have never whistled
your own tune to me
We both know
it would never ring true
So instead
you will pretend
you never said
you are disappointed
and in return
I will pretend
I never

Heard

I used to write about love

Yearning
Destructive
Wrenching
Unrequited

Scrawling out
what was not inside

Now I write about

Faith

Our father
who art in his favourite chair
trepidation be thy name
Thy word be obeyed
Thy bidding be done
in front of company
as it is in the kitchen
Give us this day
our daily nod
and forgive us our opinions
as we forgive those
that belittle us
And lead us not into an empty marriage
but deliver us from the mundane
For thine is the roof we live under
the mortgage and the car payments
until we leave this house forever

Allmen

There I go again
Putting the I'm in
imposter
Weaving
into the word
all my doubts
about my worth

Creating from
three syllables
a life sentence
that stretches
from birth
to another death
of my self
The word drawn
as a knife
over my wrists

Imposter

I know my heart
sometimes
beats black blood

I know my thoughts
riddle my brain
with bullets

I know my soul
strives
and fails
and fails
and oh how it fails

I know how
unlovable I am

And will always be grateful
no one else knows me
quite as well
as I do

Unlovable

Scarlett
When I see you
my vision tinges
with hot envy
'til it blinds me
A rush of anger
at the beauteous cape you wave
before my eyes

Cardinal
A memory of you
prickles my skin
leaks from my wounds
Beads of desire for me to suck at
the familiar iron flavour
a guilty pleasure on my tongue

Rose
Your flowery words
worm their way under my skin
Thorns of longing
slivered deep in my palms
I tweeze away at
all that could have been

Red
The raw meat of me
butchered for your approval
Eyeing the choicest cuts
Slicing between the joints and flesh
like I am the path of least resistance
Snatching up the first fruits
Leaving the heart to rot

Garnet
The wine of me
swirling round your glass
Splashing over the rim
You are drunk on my adoration
Your lips
Your teeth
stained with me
A small comfort to know
I will linger with you

Crimson
The vein of me
a darkened shadow
snaking under the surface
Spidering my eyes
Poisoning my vision
I am so clumsy
Constantly slicing myself open
on your sharpened edges
Spilling out
I am left faded

Pink and Pining

I forgave too soon
Did not give you a chance
to apologize

Now this carte blanche
This fresh start
is undeserved

And you think we are even
That what is done is
now forgotten

But I can not forget

I am reminded every time
my mind opens
its big fat mouth

Every time I hear
your voice in my head
the hurt returns

I know your lies
in a place deeper than my skin
Where I can not cut them out

And now I have robbed myself
of ever hearing you say
the words

I'm Sorry

This paper relic
This long form indulgence
where I wallow
Sink into
this ink
that flows
as slow
as a quagmire
Sucking at
my feet
my brain
my heart
Pulled under
the deep blue horizon line
Swept past
the yielding sign
the warning sigh
that I have been
led astray

And though this scratching
might disguise
it can not erase
the blatant lies

You Wrote On Me

I whipped myself raw
Chest crisscrossed with penitent stripes
the tears I rained down
upon my chest

And out from between my legs
your life slipped away
in a flood of blood
too vast for your microscopic body

You
Drowning
in all my guilt and shame
For I was unable
to accomplish the one task
I was designed for

I collected you
in a plastic cup
my child
for it was the only way
I would ever hold you

Only once
were you clutched
to the breast
that would not nourish you
Then surrendered
to some unknown
unmarked grave
And though most
did not know
you existed
my dear one
I will never forget
your flicker of life
that began and ended

In 2005

She hops
along the fence top
flicks her tail like a lure
tempting the slinking cat
They play at ignoring one another
though neither can think
of anything else

He creeps closer
twitching with desire
half hidden
intention plain

She sings a chipper tune
prays to draw him away
from breaking
her delicate future

Nest Egg

Your lies spread
like crab grass
underground

How will we ever
root out all the

Bad Theology

There is no peace
in his quiet

He is the eye of the storm
He is the riptide
He is smoking ashes

And I am on the edge waiting
To be blown away
To be dragged under
To be burned by
his rekindled

Fury

How can one sentence
slink
so softly
yet slice
so severe

Twisted Language

The ideal is non-existent
you are lovely just the way you are
Intelligent
Capable
Beautiful
Perfectly and wonderfully made
Pass it on

The ideal exists
but you are lovely the way you are
Intelligent
Capable
Beautiful
Imperfectly though wonderfully made
Pass it on

The ideal exists
but you are lovely the way you are
Capable and
Imperfectly though wonderfully made
Pass it on

The ideal exists
but you are loved
Imperfectly though wonderfully made
Pass it on

The ideal exists
You are imperfect
Pass it on

You are not enough

Broken Telephone

What life
can my words offer
when her definition is
words weaponized
When a father can explain
God ordained
this torture
When daddy spells out
love with belts
Interprets sparing the rod
as a spoiled child

How do I decipher
the platitudes they give
when she is told
she is strong enough
to endure this pain
For God does not give
more than we can handle
Even though she rests in pain
waiting to die
Wanting it
Begging for mercy
from the agony of existence

Pity her of little faith
surely that must be the reason
she has not been granted
a reprieve from this same God
they claim was the one
who smote her
with all manner of

Afflictions

I was just a child
Sunday school singing
with fingers steepled
The church is the people
when I was reborn
in a basement

Or should I say
constructed
Became a beam
in the building
Though I sat
criss cross applesauce
there unfolded in me
the knowledge that
this unbreathing building
was but a shell
The real meat of the gospel
sat in its seats

So I read the people like books
Hummed them like hymns
Whispered them like secrets
Learned them like my lesson
Clutched them like pearls

With them
my frame was formed
Plastered with their purpose
Patched with passages
plucked from the context heap
Twisted into shape
Spun and sanded
to wear away my
rough edges
until I was worn thin

My form frail from
chipping away
at what I was permitted to be
Forced against
the grain of my nature
Erected
on a fault line
where the land
shifts and shutters
beneath me

Still
my defences have not crumbled
though I stand sloped
in a village of people
where many a teetering temple
aught to be

Condemned

Chivalry was a tool

Maybe a weapon
A means of keeping us weak
Softened by a façade

Not that weakness is forged
by doors held open
or paying for meals
But because
chivalry was put on
A mask
hidden behind
Worn only for a time
Covering a face
that might be cruel
Shielding eyes
always searching
for the next best thing

By the time
we came to see
the peeling edges
the strange mismatched
colouring across a hairline
the unnatural perfection
of unblemished cheeks
it was already too late

We had been
lured in
too close to escape
Doors slammed shut
by the same hands that
once beckoned us through
Ceilings
we had been told
were designed for
our own protection
Lowered
So we bash our heads
as we crane our necks
to see the stars

Those bills they picked up
now collected as a debt
and we owe them
something more valuable
than a dinner
or a show

We have given ourselves
bound to them
A knot
not easily undone

We were
fooled by flowers
tricked by tenderness
duped by decency
and caught
in the trap of

Chivalry

There was a longing in me
to connect to him
to feel the closeness
of another
And I wanted him
with a physical craving

But there was shame
in that wanting
because I had been told
a woman was not designed
for that kind of ache

A woman was
to be the object
To be taken
Followed
Worshiped

I was not meant
to have these thoughts
To crave his touch
To dream of him
Only to wake up cold
and shaking
when he is not

Near Me

My sin is in
not fighting harder
against this body
I was given
Of giving up
without fleshing out
my fat

Condemned
by a pastor
who calls me fallen
for not fitting into
a size 2

Held in contempt
for attempting to love
these unlovable
love handles

Convicted for not
blowing them away
with my blonde
bomb shell body

You would think
they might thank me
for the weighty ways
my brick of a body
has not been whittled down
to a stumbling block

Instead I am chastised
for the audacity
of being

Seen

Why bother
creating unique
fingerprints
if I am expected
to conform
to the mould
of every
other

Woman

Lay a sheet of paper beneath me
and I will bleed on command
if it will prove our suffering
If it will teach you what it means
to be a woman
For I am able to pluck the splinters
of this life from my hands at will
There are so many stories
to tweeze out
and I have collected
the shards of sadness
from my sisters
Gore springs from my fingers
Floods the page
Puddles in the margins
where I am told
our blood belongs

Lay a bedsheet beneath me
and I will bleed on command
if it will prove my worth
If it will encourage them to keep me
For I can sacrifice the blood of a dove
pretending to be untainted
even as they lay spoil to
my body
my mind
my soul
For if there is one thing we have learned
from our years of pandering
it is that reality matters less
than the flimsy red tents
they erected
out of decades of

Faked Bedsheets

The red sea
rests between us
I have placed it there
one tear at a time

I could walk to you
on top of its waters
Still you would insist
they be split in two

For no matter whether
I am parted
or passed over
I will never be
the right kind of

Miracle For You

We all saw
the single snapshot
of a tiny boy's lifeless body
on a beach

That picture
was not clipped and collected
Instead we will do our best
to forget
how crisis conflicted
with our own conscience

For he was not
the type of child
we enjoy grinning at
The ones who's
brilliant swimsuits
are an extension
of sunny spirits

No
This child was dark
His skin
His clothing
His lungs
waterlogged

And we looked away
Quickly now
Before the toddler's torso
replaces in our brains
all the happy sandcastles
and joyous family vacations
we saved up for
instead of saving a life

We volley our points
back and forth
Debating his life
like it was no more than
a ball served over a net
Only a game to us
Losing barely even
stings our pride

We want to believe
beaches are
OUR birthright
Sandcastles are
OUR heritage

We can not have
our Christian culture
blemished by the
fearful flotsam
of one ill-fated crossing
or let compassion
muddy the waters
when we have worked
so hard to keep
our white sand beaches
pristine

We have cultivated the belief
that only those born
on these shores
should be able to
leave their mark here

Never mind
a single wave
could wipe out
all we have worked for
as easily as
water fills in the divot
where a toddler's body
found its final
resting place

Instead
we have the privilege
to take the hand of our own
pink and perfect children
pack that tiny brown body
back in the boat
he came in on
Scroll past
his family's suffering
and push it all
back out to

Sea

Standing upon
pillars we erected to support
our own self righteousness
we hoisted statues
in our own image
Carved from curated
bleached blocks of history
Held up our
marble Bibles
sand blasted
to remove every
last speck of colour

We stripped
this once vivid
technicolor gospel
this rich religion
down to a
monochromatic monument
so many long years ago
we are left with
no memory of it
being anything other than

Lilly White

The Israelites
were likewise upset
Moses tore down their

Golden Calf

At the threshold
of our city
is a barred gate
Guarded
to keep us safe
while we wait
for a saviour

Why open
for only a donkey
plodding patiently
these two thousand years
around our defences
No wonder
The hinges no longer budge
Fused tight
from the salt wet dripping
of our disappointed tears

We wanted majesty
Anticipated
a strong stallion
Believed the time had come
for our rescue
We cut branches
way too early
leaving us clutching
withered twigs
Hosanna catches
in dry throats
Parched from
neglect of water
while waiting for wine

And we haven't
learned our lesson
these many decades

This year again
a colt will come to our door
Not a bucking bronco
to kick at our
whitewashed oppression

Somehow this
turned over triumph
is once again
a surprise
and instead of following
the lead of a humble King
we have decided
it will do
to pursue a flashy

Gilded Ass

These bodies have been our offering
The first fruits
given
if not willingly
then taken
Told our free will
is not truly free
Told of the price of duty
the cost of needs
of reaping what we sow
when we sow temptation

More than our tithe is taken
out of unblemished breasts
and thighs
and reluctant pleasures
First bloodletting
rituals performed
Our remains divvied up
among the priests
for their own consumption

For our bodies are not our own
We have no right to our Nos
and NOT NOWs
and you're HURTING MEs

And though we keep bleating for mercy
we receive no year of

Jubilee

I never claimed
to be a prophet

It is just that
your sins
are so very

Predictable

I tried to say
Father forgive them
they know not what they do
but the words will not come
They stick fast in my throat
for I am not Jesus
and neither are they
Now their guilt
and my shame
still remain

Unforgiven

It could always be worse
is the motto of the oppressor
Hoping you will forget
it could also be

Better

2 become 1 and = 4
sometimes 3...5 even 10
It doesn't add up
Won't compute
You know
the equation is wrong
but they tell you
math and science lie
1+1 still equals 1
1 head
1 master
1 truth
0 doubts

(His needs)
Complete the brackets first
if there is not enough time
to finish the rest of the problem
it's okay
No worries
At least the important part is done
Now multiply by 0

A letter arrives
addressed to you
but in his name
Mrs. Man Manson
Suddenly you are 0/2
Your 1ness missing
A dropped integer
Multiplied by 0

They teach new math now
but that is a slippery slope
The curve of change so sharp
The algorithm is all off
The coefficient unfamiliar
Better multiply by 0

The rate of inflation has changed
They are taxing us to death
and we have already paid
more than our fair share
They split the bill equally
though we have not eaten
Yet your debts are
already in the red
Set on a sliding scale
of never enough
Multiplied by
whatever number suits their fancy

Find the circumference by multiplying by π
As the diameter increases
the value depreciates
Mass + time = worthlessness
The square root of ½ of who you used to be
An infinitely repeating pattern
Multiplied by 0

Oh one of small faith
a fraction of what it used to be
Half as loved
Twice as burdened
Never enough
Empty of value

Multiply by 0

God created woman
And He said that she was good
Her breasts
Her hips
Her curves
Her clitoris
are good

Then damnation came
With its coverings
and its knowledge
and its evil
and that same body
is proclaimed
no longer good
A temptation
A stumbling block
A trap

Striving starts
The work of breaking
the curse begins
Building plows
Harnessing beasts
Creating machines
to ease the burden placed on them
Doing all that can be done
to recreate the garden
Restore Eden
but not Eve

She must bear the brunt
of those pronouncements
Lean into her consequences
No soothing for the sorrow
No safety in childbirth
No sliver of skin uncovered
Crushed
under the heels of husbands
and fathers
and Pastors
as they ride their tractors
Spewing pesticides and lies
Culling her blessings
Cultivating her curses
Reminding her of her lot
Telling her it is justice
That she earned it
that it is good

It Was Good

I am still quite dizzy
Reeling
as if from a blow

They are splitting us
Hacking at the joints
Sorting us in kind
Body
Spirit
Mind
And they thought that it was good

But our body is divided against itself
We can no longer stand
and all the king's men
can't put us together again
So maybe it's time to give
the ladies a try

However
I suspect it's already too late
The shell was shattered
Blood emptied down the drain
The fat has been rendered
Holy water boils in the pot

We could have fed the masses
but we were all out of salt
The message gone rancid
poisoning the stock

This is my body broken
This is my spirit drained
This is my mind spinning

Who has eyes left to see
Who has ears that can hear
Who are the hands and feet

We traded them for blindfolds
Hands clamped over ears
Feet spinning us in circles
'til we are all quite

Dizzy

I painted pain
in deep red stripes
on the doorposts
of my life
Praying grief
would pass over

Still
an angel of death
set down
on my home
Paid no respect
to boundaries set
with bricks I formed
with the mud of
my own labour

That dark demon
stole into soul
Crept off with
my first-born love
Robbed me sightless
squinting past
a heavy fog of tears
Streaming through
the streets
in search of peace
Finding shattered pieces
Promises broken

Mine was not
the sole life
laid waste
The alleys were packed
with sorrowful wanderers
scared from
death's deep wounds

And though
the sharp heartbreak
will not let me escape
it does help
ease the burden
finding another

Hand to Hold

I prayed

I prayed with stomach empty
My heart and gut
crying out to be filled
Salt and ashes
smudging my features

From mud and dust I came
and my sludgy soul
felt the pull of returning
to the soil

Tears of blood
streamed like rivers
Yet my companions slept
Could not abide the hour of agony
Did not understand my desire
to relinquish this cup

It remained in my hand
Hollow
for the 40 days
I wandered
dust coated and dry
Alone
except for the times
he tempted me

Strength was always fleeting
even my strength of mind
Yet this cup has not been taken

This Thorn is Still in My Side

Forgiveness
was meant to transport me
past the point
of caring what you think

Instead
it sent me careening
Hurtling down the rails
towards an unknown destination

What might I have found
if I had stayed on track
until I arrived at
your apology

Where might we
have ended up
if pre-emptive forgiveness
had not skipped

Your Connection

I was born into the Church
Created
Formed
Birthed again and again
Pushed out

There is a difference
you see
between giving life and
life giving
Like the difference between
figs and apples
The first fruits
ground up
Fed to me
Here comes the airplane
into my mouth
so that from the very start
the knowledge of evil and good
was a part of me

Evil and good
Evil and goo
Evil and go

Go
Flee from the Devil
Or was he to flee from me
Clearly one of us should be running

But the only thing my muscles remember
is the pain of growth
and the agony of birth
that presented me with
birthright without rights
Built for me a red tent
Sent me out into the desert
to wander my forty days alone

And I am tempted

Tempted too forget
I was created
for so much

More Than This

Forbidden words

Like stolen oxygen
drawn into lungs
too tight to hold them

Pugged up

Congested

Covered in paper masks
designed to stop my spreading

Lines coughed out of me
in ragged gasps
onto spittle flecked pages

Drawn thin

Wheezing through
clenched teeth

Stuttered sentences
deprived of freedom
abandoned all hope

Take one last
scratchy shuttering breath

Then shrivel up and

Die

I have learned to quarantine
my whole life
Putting pieces of myself
on lockdown
Containing my
contagious questions

They told me
I should open up more
That I was ready
That they could cleanse my doubts
Inject me with oblivious assurance
Only wanting
my investments
my compliance
my labour

They did not care
my soul was suppressed
my faith compromised
and I would never survive the

Second Wave

Silly Girl
the stars say
We taught you
how to wish
but you learned
the way to

Pray

He offered the ease of plenty
Our hollow insides forever full

He offered us protection
Our bodies spared the ache of toil

He offered worldly power
We thought we could justly rule

So instead of receiving Angels
we welcomed

The Devil Through Our Door

True love waits
and waits....

and waits...
and waits......
and waits
and
   waits...

and waits...
      and waits....

and waits..
 and waits....
   and waits...

and waits...
 and waits...
and
waits...
and waits....
   and waits....
and waits...

and waits..
   and waits.
   and waits
until there is
nothing left

Worth Waiting For

Simply living
in Babylon
does not make
us its

Captives

I may not have managed
to carry my cross

But I've got a snake on a stick
and every time you bite
I look it in the eye
and the poison
is sucked
from my veins

Snakes in the Wilderness

Exodus

I stand in liminal
not knowing what way
the grief will turn

Will the rush of blood
sweep my feet out
wash me off skull rock
hurtling toward
a resurrection that feels
too heavy a curtain
to tear in two

Lament lingers in the darkness
Fear stands sentry at the grave
And though my cries
call out as thunder
still the boulder
has not

Rolled Away

Have we forgotten

We follow a God
who would rather
die on a cross
than nail others to it

Have we forgotten
the meaning of

Sacrifice

Stumbling out
into the wilderness
felt like being exiled

But the longer we spend
outside of their
spectacle of a sanctuary
the more we feel like we

Escaped

If I had not
found myself in
the wilderness

The wilderness
would have found
its way

Inside of Me

Sure
you produced
plenty of fruit

To bad it was all
next to useless

Crab Apple

Oh me of little faith
For this mustard seed
is not able
to move mountains

The only might
it can muster
will barely force
one feeble foot
in front of

The Other

You tried to crucify
all the wrong in me
and there was plenty
Though my sins
were not what you saw

You displayed
my nakedness
hung from a cliff
wind whipped
skin raw

If I told you
I was thirsty
would you offer me
bitter wine on a stick
Surely not
For why would I be given
as much as our Lord

And if I were to cry
Father why
Would he show up
to answer me
Certainly no
for he is only human
and I have already
left that question
uninterpreted at his door

Though I do not deserve
either your hate or your mercy
still my dripping request
falls from my face
splashes in the dirt
mingles with the spit

Then He comes
Lifts me down from the rock

Collects the mud in His palm
Applies paste to my eyes
Sends me out
to wash the scales away

Imagine my surprise
when I see the people
unchanged in the light of day
Still dirty
Still angry
Still afraid

But I can see
we are not so different
We are both hiding
many scars
Only the trappings
are changed
when we dress in our
Sunday best

And I want to say
it is finished
But those words
do not ring true
Instead I will offer up
forgiveness
For they know not
what they do

Scales

Now that the world
is illuminated
with electric answers
bright with powerful
currents of compassion
we discovered
what was hidden
in the paltry gaslight

Tell me how
we can forget
the way the light
revealed the stains and cracks
and return to the
fearful margins
once we know
what dangers lurk

In the shadows

I lost my voice

I searched long and hard
Under steeples and structures
Behind altars and intentions
Down isles and alleys
Yet it was nowhere to be found

Giving up the chase
I surrendered myself
to the loss
Sat down
in the wilderness

And there
cracked and dusty
parched and panting
starved and scratchy
I found my voice
where it no longer
had any place to

Hide

Scored and sectioned
by circumstance
I take up knowledge
The sharpened spoon
to scrape the bitter pith
from my soul

Once
Twice
Three times
I am plunged into
the boiling tempest

That brutal baptism
draws some of the
sourness from my skin
But not all
Never all
For that would be
a removal of
my deepest nature

And though this life
still stings
there is enough
scalding sweetness
to steep slowly in
to permeate even
the toughest parts

With the shrivelling of time
sharpness mellows
and I find that this
resentful rind
has been redeemed

These parts
once worthless
transformed
Turned into
a tangy treat
My essence preserved

And your mouth will not
soon forget

The flavour of Me

The glorious future
That make-believe mystery
where all mistakes are mended
Inventive expectations perfected
and our sins are swept
under the rug

The glorious future
An elusive dream
of all things made new
Where the passage of time
is a tunnel

Dig us out of this mess
to that projected hour
The hand never traveling
far from home
Gravity spinning
back to the beginning
where all things are
made great again
Burying the myriad reasons
we left in the first place
Tried to get the hell out of dodge

This longing
for a glorious new future
under an old sun
drives us through the groove
of a retro song on repeat

So if I were to divine
where we will find ourselves
in 2025
I imagine it will look
an awful lot like

1984

Go home
they say

Like it is a game of Trouble
Like they have landed on the same space you occupy
Like they want to claim this spot as their own
Like they are trying to put all their little pegs in a row
Like there can only be one winner
Like they are afraid you might take the prize
Like this game is fun for you
Like you have not already been sent home before
Like they think you will be safe there
Like faithfulness matters less than the pop of the dice
Like saying sorry erases blame
Like they did not cause the trouble
Like they do not make the rules
Like loosing again and again will make you give up
Like you should want to quit
Like they can force you to

Go Home

These wishes will wait
They sleep like death
under the snow
and dream of spring
with its joyful tears
and longing embrace
when time stoops
to beckon
Fall's forgotten seeds
from the earth

These wishes will wait
disappointed in false starts
Mourning the many
withered possibilities
Holding on to brittle hopes
with faith
Always faith
that one will take root
Will burst forth
to create offspring of its own
carried soft
upon the breeze
for us to catch
and wish upon a
like a

Dandelion Seed

I shed the shuttering
dull brittle
layers I was clothed in
Stripping off
constricting skin

He told me moulting
makes me a snake
For only a snake
would slough him off this way
Called me a deceiver
Said he ought to
crush the evil in me
under his heel

It shook me
to see his boot
poised over my head
and my unfamiliar body
weary from the
turmoil of transformation
craved the safety
of the sky
While his fervour for
destruction over discipleship
brough down
pressing judgment

But a jolting urge to escape
pumped fear
throughout me
and I found myself
spreading surprising wings
and bursting into

Flight

She left the fold
Fled from the pasture

They could not understand
why she would abandon
their green grass
their quiet water
their warm Son

And she tried to return
To drink and be satisfied
To rest in their rocky pen
But she could not be still
Was unable to find peace
in their pasture
Did not blend in
with the flock
even in the shadowy valley

They would not believe
her bleating
refused to listen
to her frightened warnings
as she ran for the hills
Still she hoped they would follow
Prayed the Shepherd would come
rescue her from the cliff
carry her back to the meadow
But only when
the flock was safe
and there was no longer
a wolf hidden

In Their Midst

As children
we were taught
not to touch wild animals
That there was danger
in drawing close to
unpredictable beasts

Yet no one thought to mention
the wildest animal
we would encounter
is the vicious greed
of an arrogant man
who feigns

Domestication

If you didn't
know better
you would say
nothing grows
in the wilderness

Then I would tell you
look harder

For a stark landscape
lends way
to a deeper stretching
An age defying resilience
Sharpened understanding

The desert is where
unrelenting heat
cures enduring beauty

And hope
can spring up
out of

Stones

I wonder how many wonders
I have missed by mere

Meters

We once believed
we were the centre
of the universe

Strangely
we still do

Axis Shift

He put to death
the parts of him
my weary heart
was seeking

Yet I never mourned
since his
haunting ghost
was ever so convincing

He raged and howled
the very same
as he had
always done

And with him dead
I did not feel
I was any

Less Alone

On the tip of my tongue
sits a bullet
Locked and loaded
it clicks against my teeth

My aim it true
I'm a real sharpshooter
This is not a hollow point
I am not aiming to kill
though I sure am itching
Cause there is a bright red bullseye
painted on your puffed-up chest
and you have peppered
me with pebbles
my entire life
So if one more stone is thrown
I know I could claim
self defense

Come on
just try me
and then you will see
what I can do
My patience has been worn thin
and my restraint is so weary

My mouth has been feeling

Trigger Happy

Deconstruction
is a dirty word
and rightly so
it is a dirty job
Difficult and frightening
because you never know
what you will find
when you open a wall

The electrical
meant to shed light
to power our life
is often jumbled crossed wires
A fire hazard of live current
Shocking how messy it can get

We broke down
those crooked frameworks
Saw the cracks
in our foundation
and knew that this
foolish faith
was not so sound

Because we had learned
your lessons about
how impossible it is
to remain standing
on shifting sand
And knew the tune
About what happens when
the rains come down and
the floods come up
We understood that
if we had any hope
for safe shelter
we would need
to tear down these houses
Rebuild them anew
Bring them up to code

We set to work
constructing a new faith
with a sturdy foundation
A new blueprint of love
A centred set of level ground
An open concept home
All while using
that same old

Cornerstone

They were taught a marching tune
A bitter melody
chocked full of thoughts of war
and they sharpened their sword words
girded their loins
strapped on breastplates of self righteousness
held up shields of blind faith
their vision obscured
by helmets of their assured salvation
Fear focused their minds on protection
Safety for everything and nothing
A fragile care for the life
they had built
on the backs of the broken
Those wills they bent
for their own good
when good was for one
not for all

Husbands kissed their wives
and hummed that marching tune
as right foot
right foot
right foot
led them off to war
Too many pivots in the same direction
and they were pointing home
Lowering their weapons at the enemy
their own sons and daughters

I remember the lullaby
he sang as he took aim
The simple tune that filled the air
passed down like a curse
to the seventh generation
an anthem meant to soothe
and remind me to
always be good
and kind
and gentle
and mouldable
yet virtuous
and above all
pure
This sleepy tune never lit up his eyes
the way the marching song
about the blood always could

He ran his fingers through
my long blonde hair
my glory
and whispered sweet nothings in my ear
Whispered that I was sweet
and I was nothing
Then that Christian soldier fired
His verses filled with gun powder
whistled past my face
a superficial wound
upon my cheek
and so I turned
to him

The Other

He who has ears
let him hear
Let him bravely pull the plugs
that have stopped up his listening
and let the strained sound
of voices drowning in despair
wash over him
in salty waves

He who has a tongue
let him choke
on his own medicine
That silt grit pill
so hard to take
no matter how many
sugary apologies
it is coated with
The broken promises
coughed up in ragged gasps
upon the shore

He who has feet
let him wander
the rickety boardwalk
Awash with destruction
Riddled with death
and creatures that sting
Where barefoot strolls
are not recommended
Take care where you
place your path
when tender toes
have been given
no protection

He who has breath
let him cry out
A booming warning
to watch your step
Avoid the broken boardwalk
Leave it to rot
Abandon it to the storm
Relinquish it to the wind
that whistles into lungs
Filling them with
salt fresh air
Clearing the gunk
from heads bowed in reverence
allowing them to sing
a sweat sorrowful song of

Surrender

Balance the good book
upon your mind
Keep your graceful posture
directed towards the Lord

But I am clumsy
Not upright enough
Unsteady in my movement
No perfect poise
to stop its slipping
Hurried steps of correction
are not enough to steady it

It teeters and tumbles
Pages flutter as it falls
But does not shatter
Does not tear
Is not broken

Instead I can see inside
Read printed passages
that had never before
permeated my brain
Had not sank through
my thick skull
when my only aim
was balancing the good book
upon my crown

Now I can see
wondrous words written
Explaining the many rich ways
there is so much more
To being a lady than

Posture

If you judge a book
by its cover
a woman's supple leather
would convince you
she was soft
That the story
she will tell you
is light with joy
A happy fantasy
A romantic comedy
Unless you take the time
to look inside her
Feel her pages
against your skin
Listen to the words
printed in the worry lines
around her eyes
Run your finger over
the puckered places
where her tears have fallen
You will not know
the hardness in her
How unfortunate the rips
and careless folding
she has sustained
How tragic
the many red herrings
thrown her way
Only once you have read her
will you understand
the trust it has taken
for her to open up to you and

Lend You Herself

She sits
and scrapes her skin
like Job
feeling his pain
understanding his loss

I sit with her
Silent
In Shiva
For there are no words
that would bring comfort

When she breaks the silence
like she has been broken
I offer my tears
Salt for her wounds

I fear they do not
bring cleansing
Encourage no healing
They only sting
her raw lesions

Adding to Her Agony

We believed our roots
were made of sterner stuff

Maybe we were
Simply planted in

Softer Soil

She sings their songs
Cuándo me levantará el Señor de la desesperación
When will the Lord lift me from despair

The melody mournful
though harmonic with hope

She carries their tunes
floating wistful across the margins
She will bring them here
word by word
Pieces of them drifting on the air
into the ears of a country that
refuses to give their bodies

Refuge

When we believe
the poor have
the same opportunities
as we do
it makes it
so much easier
to blame them
for not tugging harder
on those boot-straps
instead of noticing
they have

Bare Feet

Just because our skin
is white as sugar
does not mean we are sweet
More likely they are sick
from too much of us

Plugging in like a
pretty pink Himalayan salt lamp
does not make us the
salt and light
We might just be dull and salty

Milky flesh does not make us
fresh and wholesome
It only means we will curdle
when life
gives us vinegar

Growing up as white as sheep
does not mean we will
always be kept safe by the shepherd
Instead we would follow the flock into danger
and must be shorn to be useful

Being mistaken for a snowman
does not mean we are cool and cheery
Maybe we are just cold
and the first heat we take
will leave us in a puddle

Floating around like a fluffy
cloud in the sky
does not make our ideas lofty
It only means we have farther to fall
and eventually we will

Being white as a ghost
does not make us holy
Though it might mean
we are haunting and a bit fearful
even though they can see through the many

Ways We Are White

My brother from
another mother
I say
Because we share
the same last name

His dark eyes turn
toward me sadly
and he replies
Except your family
would have owned mine

It should not have taken
his words
to make me realize
the way his family identity
was removed from them
Cut from their line
like a label snipped
from a shirt collar
and a new name
placed upon them
just the same as
stitching a monogram on

A Possession

Moses is still crying
Let my people go
Harriet is still crying
Let my people go
Colin is still crying
Let my people go

But where will they go
when they already stand
in the land
of milk and honey
Where will they turn
when we have turned
their own home
against them
How far can they run
when there is no
place to run to
and they are almost
out of air
whispering

I Can't Breathe

For we have been wearing
our designer sackcloth
'til it has become
the latest trend
Selling our inheritance
Squandering our fortune
in wasteful extravagance

Our deep pockets
conceal the matches
we used to light
this fire now licking
at our heels

We spoke of exclusive sneakers
to those who had
blisters on their feet
and asked each other
what she was wearing
like it had bearing
on the condition of her soul

Now strip off your shoes
Walk barefoot
through the rubble
Let your soles feel
the agony of being unable
to walk freely
in your own land

Scoop up the ashes
of the cities
we would rather burn
than share

Smear lament like soot
upon your face
an admission to the world
of the grimy crimes
you are complicit in

Let your body shake
with a death rattle of weeping
as you destroy
the biased lies within

And let your tears
flood the streets
until the waters
run deep enough
for you to be plunged into

A New Baptism

We spray painted NO ROOM
across the welcome to Jericho sign
We sit listening to
their tortured trumpets
The wailing cry
blasting from every
screen in the city
We watched
as they were pressed
Squashed down under
the Mason-Dixon line
And we know of how
the Ohio river
piled up
Under their feet

How many times has
their mourning procession
circled this city
How many days has
their lumbering lament
passed these blasted gates
while they march and grieve
trailing behind the Ark
of years of testimony

Do we not melt
in remorse and trembling
with the knowledge that
right is on their side
For they have taken
off their sandals
they have walked
on holy ground
and we can attest
to the oppression
we measured out
with whips
and bullets
and laws
and knees

So tremble at their trumpet
Gather your loved ones
in this redeeming room
For some have tried to
cover the scouts with flax
They have tied this
red rope from the overpass

We know the shout is coming
that the system was
built too tall
and we can only pray
to be Rahab
when we feel

God's Justice Fall

The devil is in the details
Satan stands by the slander
of a Black man's character
so white eyes can ignore
yet another soul
snuffed out

If Christian breath is not
as easily taken
by the madness of our
blue murder for hire
If wounded pride
is enough instigation
to wield whiteness
as a weapon
If a man can kneel on a neck
more casually than kneeling
at the cross
feigning innocence
while lynching Black lives
deceit runs deeper than our skin and

Lucifer is in Our Lies

We are miserable comforters
Refuse to be ugly criers
Because what could be
more important
than maintaining
our perfect façade
while inside
we are crumbling

Why not also be judged
by the beauty of our tears
as if only
retouched tragedy
is worthy of being seen

If every action
has an equal
and opposite
reaction
does that mean
that your ugly acts
must be met
with pretty pain
or does the fact
that you have
dressed up your sins
in their Sunday best
give us the right
to shed our

Ugly Tears

Mercy

What is this word
unfamiliar to her tongue
that sits heavy
unspoken
Like a foreign language I am
Ill-equipped to interpret

She has no experience
of mercy for me to draw on
No metaphor or simile
will explain what it is
when she has
struggled under a lifetime
of unrelenting burden

How much can a soul take
before it breaks

Less than what she was given
For she is soul-broken
from years of unrelenting misery
Still mercy remains
elusive

It is not hiding under hospital beds
She has looked
Nor sampled in the biter pills
she has swallowed
Once she believed
she heard notes of it
floating in a sirens song
only to be dashed again
against the rocky shore

Now I cry with her
the salty sting on our cheeks
an offering to exchange for
mercy

Still it is evasive
How will she cage it

By trapping it in a car
that sits running in a closed garage
or pinning it down with knives
cutting deep
to release it from her veins
or standing in traffic
eyes closed against the impact
hoping they will not swerve
or pouncing upon it unaware
as it hides at the bottom
of a deep ravine

The word mercy
sounds like death to her
Oblivion is the only
leniency she can lean in to

So I whisper mercy in tongues
praying there is an interpreter
to offer a simple explanation
that will not require
more patience
more agony
more sacrifice
before she is given
a lesson in

Mercy

We staked a claim
to civility
and to land
and to the lives we
fought to posses
Calling them
Savage
Barbaric
Uncivilized

We focused on the
scalping of a man
as if it were
the epitome of violence
Pretended that
severing him
from his children
amputating his livelihood
stealing his history
raping his land
and his wife
was not the embodiment
of evil

We feigned innocence
Pretended genocide
was a synonym for
progress
and imagined that history
would look favourably
at this Holocaust
See it as
a revolution

Yet when they dared
attempt to shed
the noose we hung
around their throats
our voices called out
across generations

But look
how generously
we gave them
the things they

Never Wanted

He took more
than their innocence
Ripped out
their trust
Trampled on the
idea of family
Stole their belief
that love could be
unconditional
and given by God

Once he was
done taking
the church swooped in
and stole the rest
Told them they should
pray their way
out of shame
out of brokenness
out of harms way

Then cast them out
set them adrift
without an anchor
no paddles
no sail
and blamed them
for the way the
waves threw them

But Jesus
walked towards them
across the water
Through the storm
was still raging

He came
Not as a father
but as a stranger
a would be sister

Though the tempest
did not subside
like the church
claimed it would
they were instead given
tools to help them
weather it out

Ores to row
a raft to escape
life vests to
keep them afloat
and a friend
to help paddle
through dark and
angry waters
as that stranger
shone a brilliant light
towards the

Distant Shore

The wind was my teacher
Its gentle caress
whispered tendrils
of my own hair
across my face
and I leaned into
the pleasant reprieve
I laughed as I drew back my hair
collected it in a band
so the wind would
no longer tangle it
But the wind did not need
hair to caress me with
its warm breath was sufficient
and I was lifted up
as it tenderly
kissed my neck

I learned joy from the wind
the free running of
the kite I would sprint with
through the fields
at my grandparent's farm
Buoyed on a breeze
to soar high
on a sweet spring day
though spring is merely
a small portion of a year
and there are other lessons
the wind would like me to learn
for even wind
has its seasons

I learned to tremble from the wind
its untamed tornado
that uprooted the forest
behind our house
a hard lesson in
how much power
there can be
in something unseen
Fire lifted on wind's wings
fed from its own mouth
like a baby bird
beak wide and squawking
And I felt fear
flicker through me
like the tongues of flame
that licked at the forest
on the day I was born
causing my family
to greet me quickly
before fleeing to soak buildings
in the hopes they would not
scorch and crumble
on the same day
my life was unearthed

I learned patience from the wind
as it chiseled the shoreline
wielding water as its
sculpting tool
Pushing it into the cracks
Melting away the parts that are soft
I learned how much time
It takes to whittle away
a course hard thing
and I would need to wait
to find the beauty
concealed in me
like the rock pillars
resembling flowerpots
I swam to through the frigid waters
around a northern island
Formed from slow movement
of ice and wind
taking eons to carve its skin

I learned endurance from the wind
Even when it is still
it is waiting
and when it rages
I am given something to push against
Like the paddle boat I peddled
out into the ocean
Fighting against tall waves
strong enough to keep me
far from shore
There I learned
even though I could not control
the size of what
I strive against
I am capable of riding out the storm
or at the very least
I can steer my ship to
cut across the swells
building enough strength
in my legs
to carry me home
where I am sheltered from

The Lessons of Wind

The house of God is haunted
by a ghost we once thought holy
This is a spectre slowly summoned
by a tortured twisting of scripture
Poking us awake in the night
Snuffing out our candles
Lurking under the covers
Frightening us with
bedtime stories
of fire and brimstone
Rattling its chains of
Guilt and shame
until eventually
we have had enough
and we rise up
from our fitful slumber
with the need to exorcise these

Unholy Ghosts

Forgive and forget
chant the guilty
And I have forgiven
7 x 70 times

I recited the words
and tried to forget
But my body remembers
no matter how often
it has been scoured raw

Your hurts are written
in my DNA
I am reminded every time
I see a piece
of my brash body
that does not meet
your modest approval

And I hope I do not pass
Christian shame down
to my daughter
in the same way I have given her

The Shape of My Face

They have whittled
the narrow road
down to a tight rope
Yet still they balk
when we build

Cable Cars

Where is the rainbow
that promises my roads
will never be flooded
with remorse once again

This grief must have
turned it

Grey

If only we could hold onto love
as tightly as we grip our

Grudges

It is not that I am broken
I am simply leaning
and this land is not

Level

Be ye in the world
but not of it

A lofty ideal
For a people
Made of dust

I must confess
I do not know how
to be of this soil
and not toil for the
things made of earth
when even our Lord
so loved this world
that He sent
His own Son to be

Dirt

Promised Land

The desert was deemed
desolation
A wilderness given
instead of salvation
by a God we believed
would pull Their people
from one punishment
only to subject them to another

How to reconcile
with a redeemer
who offers only
perpetual purgatory

Yet what if
the desert is not damnation
Since even in the wasteland
we want for nothing

Water from a stone
Mana from dew
Quail from sky
Peace in a pillar of cloud
Rest in waiting
Courage in following fire

Sustain Your stumbling people
in a space
ripe with nothing
but restoration

Soothe Your weary worshipers
in a stark scenery
where all beauty
must be teased out of minds
unaccustomed to calm

Comfort Your leery listeners
in a lonely land
where there is learning in the liminal
as the wilds lend way
to mournful meditation

Sustain Your stumbling people
in a slow space
where bludgeoned bodies
can treat the tension of trauma
forcing leaden limbs to rest

Do not rush to the promise
even though its silhouette
is in view on the horizon
Though the soil is rich
it will take toil
to build
to grow
to cultivate

This labour is best left
to souls that have not
been mistreated
By bodies that have not
been pushed past the limits
of capacity

It is possible
those who live humbly
in the hinterlands for a lifetime
have simply been given

A Different Sort of Promised Land

Nolite te Bestardes Carborundorum

Stitched pretty
Each needle prick
pulls a tread of memory
Stretched taught
Nailed in place

For we tend to heed
what is hung
Whether it be
a wicked warning
or righteous rules

This is the latter
A reminder
to climb ladders
Stand strong on the rooftops
Cut holes in them
if that is what it takes
to get their attention

And we know they will click their tongues
Tell us
nice girls never
raise their voices
But we will still
raise ours
and our arms
and our children
Stretch them out
to embrace both the welcome
and the warning

For we will love
'til the needle tears us open
We will weave
with every colour we can find
And we will hang
our message proudly
for all to see

But we will never again
let the bastards

Bring Us Down

Keep your demons
on a short leash
they said
Train them to do
your bidding
Submit to your lead
Walk quietly by your side

I have never had a
force of will
able to bend demons
to my desire
I lacked the strength
to keep them contained

So I released them
Set them free
to explore the limits
before attempting
to cage them once more

Imagine my surprise
when some did not return
and the ones that remained
became restrained companions
Calm and faithful pets
No longer the unruly monsters
I had once feared
When trying to
rule them with

A Short Leash

I was shaken

Their twisted scripture a
live wire current
that jolted me
Kept me rooted
in troubled twitching
Sleepless nights
of tortured tossing
The voltage enough
to burn
to scar

Tongue swollen
Vision blurred
Body bent by
the force of the
pulsing poison

They thought
they could shock me
Keep me silent
Keep me blind

Instead I have learned
how much I can take
now that I have found
a space that is

Grounded

Do not deny me my mourning
Do not diminish my grief
For loss has settled
on my shoulders
as a yoke I am tasked with
carrying alone
Slowly plodding
Plowing formidable fields

Instead I ask you
to step in beside me
Lock your neck
in the harness
Push with me
against the faithful beam

Together
we can furrow
this lonely field
Cut deep ruts
of empty longing
Cast hopeful seeds
Water them
with our tears
and link arms with one another
as we watch it grow
Pain pruning our lament
into fruitful

Harvest

They hurtle labels as curses
meant to sting
to wound
Hoping one will deal the death blow

Backslider
Liberal
Socialist
Jezebel
Apostate
Heretic

Instead we choose
a label for ourselves

Exvangelical

X
The letter they rallied against

They said writing Xmas
was taking Christ out of Christmas
crossing him out
like He is nothing
Forgetting how
X stands for Christ

Now with our insertion
of an X in their label
we are only attempting
to reposition Christ in

Evangelical

I was told
this softness
made me weak

And I believed it
when the shock of you
rippled through me

Yet I found myself
able to absorb
every heavy thing
you tossed my way
and I used your stones
to make myself grow by

Displacement

I discovered folds in my sides
Creases that buckle
bent and pressed
into my flesh

I have turned myself
upside-down
and inside out
Cutting along the lines
Meeting ends together
Pleating the paper of me
until I am transformed
Turned out
Origamied into
a beautiful

New Creature

I found myself
in the page

My story had
their mark
all over it
scrawled in their
curling cursive
between the lines
of what I had written

No more

I took black ink
to all their false statements
Editing them out
of my message
Painstakingly translating
until I found my voice
Then I wrote myself
a new ending
and sent out
into the world

My Query

Do we even dare
Can our hope in healing
compel our muscles
to carry our friend
Present them to Jesus

Do we even dare
Can our faith in a miracle
lift our feet to climb
the steps to the rooftop
past the crowd

Do we even dare
Can our love for the broken
Claw our hands
to dig through
dirt ceilings
reckless in our want for change

Do we even dare
Can new understanding
convince our minds to accept
even the easier
That our failings are forgiven

Do we even dare
Can this question become a commission
to abandon our comfort
Give it to the broken
even when it requires we

Dare to Break Ourselves

I do not have a spirit of fear
though I inherited
the fabric of one
Passed down
for seven generations
until it was shoddy
Worn thin
Fraying under the needle
when I attempted to
patch it

But this is no
priceless heirloom
No worthy gift to treasure
This fear has outlived
its usefulness

So I threw
that old fear
out with the trash
and sewed myself
a new garment

Soft with kindness
Woven in love
Dyed bright with joy
Adorned with courage
A garment truly worthy
of becoming an

Heirloom

Losing you
felt frivolous
Left me wanting
Spent from spilling
precious tears

How fortunate
that every drop
turned out to be
worth its weight in

Salt

All my life I thought
of ways to make you think of me
Scheming to gain your love

All my life I thought
I needed to change myself
Attempted to hack off the pieces
that did not fit inside your box
the breasts
the thighs
the hips
the independent thought

All my life I thought
the thoughts you had for me
Words poured fast
funnelled into my mind

But it was already too full
Full of ideas
of what could be
and hopes for a love
that did not depend
on your headship
and umbrellas
and submission to a will
that shrunk me

All my life
I was wrong
when I thought
I was not good
or strong
or worthy
Because I looked
in that book
Studied its pages
Searched for these
clear words you
siphoned off

And you were right
They were clear
So clear in fact
they were transparent
Just like your motives
to disguise
the red letters
that tell me
all the truthful things
I should have believed

All my life

I see him still
in the scars that mark my soul
But not because he carved them

In their thick hardened lines
I see his healing hand
Recall the delicate way
his lips brushed
the tenderest parts of me
and how his fingers
were the ones that
stitched up my

Wounds

They told me
my fruit was rotten

They did not know
it was only Jesus
turning my water into

Wine

My world was so silent
you only needed to whisper
to make yourself heard
Your words traveled
down my ear canal
straight to my heart
You gave me
the kiss of life
Awakening my bones
to a longing I had
always suspected
was not meant for me
and inflated my lungs
with the air I needed
to fill my silent world with

Music

You are an artist
and I was in love with
your movement
from the first moment
I saw your form
Recognized your heart
right away in its style

How mine ached
when I looked at you
The pain strange
Particular to you
Different than
the agony I felt when
others looked at me
seeing something only
flat and lifeless

I was drawn to your
technique
by the longing
to see myself
though the eyes
of a master
Because I knew
before you fingers
ever brushed my cheek
that your touch
would paint over
the dullest parts of me
with vibrant brushstrokes of

Affection

I am afraid I am
not enough for you
Or more like there is too much
of me to be beautiful
The mirror mocks
as I poke the places
where time has left
thick rings around my middle
I fuss with clothing
Try to disguise
those dimpled parts

What can I do
to turn back time
To clip your tied tongue

Tell me
I alone
am so lovely I make
your head forget its grey hair

I want to draw awe from you
Make you whisper it
to all the insecure parts of me
My rounded face I gave as legacy
My heavy breasts that nursed your children
My thick thighs that root me to you

Your body has done
what your voice only hints at
Your feet tell me you will walk beside me
Your arms tell me my softness comforts you
Your laugh tells me I am your safety and
Your eyes tell me you are

Home

I do not mourn
the things I have missed
for the reasons you believe
Truly I am in love with our life
Overjoyed with the beauty
we built together

It is only that
grief still fills some spaces
that could have been better by now
I am saddened by how I missed the chance
to have already made myself into
something more glorious

For You

You used to
alight into boxes
Your happy caw
a surprise that
leapt from your throat
to make your
Mother jump and laugh

Nested in narrow
cardboard halls
Your preening pressed
against bowed walls
where you were safe
though the framework
was flimsy
and markered windows
let in no light

Your burgeoning body
was eventually unable
to origami itself
into those same
small spaces
Boxes bursting
Replacing toys with tools
Packed tight with
heavy curated works
that could not be contained

You ripped off morsels
Ravenously stuffing them
into your ears
'til your brain was full
to bursting
Vowels spilling from your mouth
Regurgitating the lessons
you were bird fed
beak to beak
Pecking at the pieces
too tough to swallow
And there was so much
to swallow

Boxes replaced by bars
meant to keep you safe
Those chaste locks
left unopened
were well intentioned
Maybe it wasn't so bad
At least you could
see the sun
from your wooden
perch swing
only swaying
back and forth
Waffling
wile the shadows
slip each day
across your chest
Playing at warmth
Flirting with freedom
And though this home
is more spacious than some
it is still a cage

But the devil you know
is better than
the one you don't
Or so you've been told
It's understandable
you were stunned
when He came
with the key
Forced that rusty gate open

For weeks you stayed still
Never setting one toe
out of line
Leary of becoming lost
Worried about the world
Frightened by the forest
Because trees are not boxes
though they're made
of the same stuff

They tried so many times
to clip your wings
but you must know
the woods are waiting
and you
were made

To Fly

If I was a tree
Trunk thick
Leaves brilliant
Branches gnarled
Roots shallow
You would have made
kindling out of me
Chopped me down
with sharpened words
Consumed me
with fiery anger
and scattered my ashes
Not even a memory
to remain

Instead I was a maple key
Lifted on comforting winds
Spinning from affection
Carried to the fertile soil
of a distant land
There I sprouted
Grew into a strong sapling
in lush ground
Reaching for the light
Tendrils drinking deeply
from the fresh stream
Clothed in the vibrant mantle of spring
Sun sweetening my veins
Savouring their shade
My weaknesses supported by the forest
where the gale cannot uproot me
and I can live

Unswayed

I wished to be stone
Hard and unrelenting
Forceful in a way that
being cut and polished
draws out beauty
to reflect the light
Strong
Enduring
Valuable

And my wish was

Granted

My heart remembers
the pull of its strings
the music it made
when I saw Yahusha clearly
for the first time

My heart remembers
the throb of my pulse
pushing the good news
through my body
healing the parts of me
that had been cut and bruised

My heart remembers
the times it was broken
All the small hurts
I wore on my sleeve
and the flush of my skin when
when my heart remembers
the ache of your lies
stitched inside me

But my heart is mended
New truth a potent salve
slowly seeping into my wounds
and though the memory of them
will forever mar my flesh
my heart remembers
that old scars
no longer

Bleed

Her hands
held fast to mine
from a time beyond
my remembering

Her thumbs
unable to rest still
Can not help caressing
the palms of
the ones she loves

Her hair
Fine like mine
A halo upon her head
A golden crown
she does not know
she deserves

Her eyes
The first to see
beauty in me
The same loveliness
she was too
far sighted
to spot in herself

Her arms
She opens so willingly
Lends them
to others
Lifting them up
over her own head

Her legs
Sometimes limping
Unable to keep pace
with her busy dreams
of places she wishes
her legs could carry her

Her backbone
Still strong and straight
supports the posture of
her character and

Her body
A wonder of wisdom
A beautiful blessing
A gift given
ever willingly by a

Mother

Could Jesus
have surrounded Himself
so closely with the 12
to fill the void
where His family
who did not
understand Him
might have been

Instead He built for Himself
a chosen family
A model of
supportive love
To show the way
the church was
designed to be

Home

We were told
our voices
were too shrill
to listen to

But maybe instead
our words were
simply too painful
for them to

Hear

All things
work together
for good
They say when
burdens fall
and strife piles up

Tell that to Job
Remind him
his tears
are good
after he has suffered
the loss of his children

Do not tell me
how he was given back
double what was taken
As if the hole
in a heart
left by a child
can be filled with
two others

Do not placate me
with promises
of an easy future
when right now
is punishing

Instead tell me
you will do good
you will share freely
you will seek justice
you will love mercy

Only then
will I know
you have an inkling of
how much work
good truly is
An understanding
of how sorrow
is not soothed
by the promise
of a happy ending

That solace is only glimpsed
in the bravery
it takes to remain
with those who suffer

That we must be
the ones
to put in the work and

Do Good

My body has been broken
by the children that
spilled from my womb
But spilled is too imprecise a word
Broken is more like it
For them
my body was torn
like a loaf of bread is torn

My body remembers
it was told
the breaking would be
my redemption
That I would be saved
through the blood
of childbirth

Every week
I am told stories
about a man whose
body was broken
Told of blood that was
shed for me
These sermons preached
from a pulpit
by a man whose body
is illiterate to sacrifice
One who has not bled
for the sake of another

Every year
I am reminded of the birth
of a savior
by a man whose skin
has not been stretched
to accommodate growing life
Whose spine has not
cracked and bent as it bore
the perpetual heaviness
of carrying a child

And I cannot help but wonder
at the climax of this story
How beautiful
How rich it could be
if it were told
by a body that remembers
One that has an intimate understanding
of the metaphor of a
body broken

For The Sake of Another

I have carried you
inside me for years
Like a child that will not
quit the womb

I swelled with you
Back aching
Skin stretching
to accommodate
your uncomfortable size

But the time has come
to disentangle you
from me
Though you might
rip and tear my centre

I know now
that I am strong
That I will heal
and if I want
to discover who
I was meant to be
I must reclaim
these spaces

Within Me

Peace
we have been told
is like a river
Quietly babbling
alongside the narrow path

But that is not
what we need peace to be

Would we not rather
it was wild rapids
we can ride on
rushing down
life's turbulent waters
Carrying us swiftly
over rocky conflict
Skimming the surface
of what is set
to cause us harm
Propelling us ever forward

Only then
when peace has performed its duty
When we have reached a space
deep and wide
with gentle grace
Only then
should peace be permitted
to be a quiet stream
Only then
will peace like a river

Sit Well With My Soul

The distance between
rejected and wanted is wide
and we drift there
Brooked
Floating someplace
close to accepted
but not embraced
The cold liquid flowing around us
has a current
Rushes downstream
tumbling past the tolerated spaces
rushing out into the ocean

The salty sea air
floods into our lungs
purifies our breath
and we know
this is where we belong
this is where we are needed
Where the fish are plentiful
and the sunlight
draws colour to our skin
An invigorating breeze
lifts our stagnant spirits
making us wonder why
we ever tried so hard
to swim

Upstream

How can God
be present in this
In my grappling
My striving
In pain
In pleasure
In the many ways
I fail
and believe God
has failed me

Yet in prayer
Drawn from my throat
in strangled sobs
Shaking supplication
Forces a fall
to my knees
I am broken hearted
Cracked open

In those spaces
between the raw
sharp edges of me
the light is finally able
to slip in
and my prayers
are illuminated
Finally reaching
the deepest spaces
where they have
never been

Present Before

Shame is given to girls
More freely than grace
More lavishly than trust
More generously than love
Ladled out
A heaping helping
Seconds and thirds
'til we are bloated with it
Obese

Shame is planted
in child minds
Wild seeds cultivated
Taking root in synapses
The once rich soil polluted
with the drug of approval
A craving for devotion
Narcotics that come at a cost
The fare paid by
submission to every whim and fancy
of the jealous and overreaching

Shame hovers behind her youth
on a wine dark winter evening
Keys clutched like a weapon in her fist
though it is already too late
Shame was slipped into her drink
hours ago
Poured down her throat
bitter and stinging
'til she was powerless against it

Shame tells her she deserves it
This is the price of poor choices
For daring to grow up
with a body like that
A form more tempting
than Eve
than Bathsheba
What did she expect
dressed in fig leaves and firs

Shame grows in a woman's belly
A remorseful blossom
inserted in her against her will
As it grows it is given names
that make it seem soft
benignly companionable
though the discomfort
of raising shame
all alone
was never her choice to make

Shame flows from her
drips down her thighs
Puddles under her feet
Slick and slippery as the slope
she was warned about
The one they slid down so long ago
Yet she must remain lofty
aloof
even when the valley
Is crowded with vast cities

She is a jezebel
who dares cast off the shackles
of shame she was bound with
A heretic for honouring
the beauty in her sister
Sinful for surrounding her
like a hedge of protection

Lead her into
the red tent
A secluded place
away from prying eyes
Strip her of her soiled name
Let it fall away
revealing the beauty
she has never embraced
and wash away the blame
that sticks to her like tar
Scour her toughened skin 'til she is

Shameless

Do the work
Find function in the body of Christ
Be the eyes
Be the hands
Be the feet
Not one piece better than another
A body built as a visionary
to reap
to sow
to go
out into all the world

But what if this body
is not a form solely fit
for the harvest
What if it held potential
for birth
Be a womb
Protect and grow
the seeds of new souls
Be the hips
set wide to make a way
for new life
Be the breasts
heavy with richness
enough to nourish the nations
A body brimming
with the possibility of encapsulating
the wonder of the miraculous

How is it
these ears never heard
a sermon extol the virtue
in these parts of

The Bride of Christ

A regular day
filled with remarkable sorrow
casts you out
upon dark waters
For a belly needs food
A body needs work
A mind needs numbing
and what could be better than
a task to accomplish all three

Move through the motions
Cast the net
Drift hollow
Watch as the mist settles
Imagine there is
no longer a shore
to return to

Then out of the gloom
a familiar voice
echoes from the distance
or maybe your memory

Cast your net on the other side

An act that ought to make
little difference
and you will prove it
For you have lost
even the strength to argue

Yet hope flashes
under the surface

For an ordinary day
might become extraordinary
Unseen movements
could be at play

Instead of believing
you will once again
come up empty
you toss vacant snares
in a new direction
and find yourself

Fishing for Miracles

There is value in the church
Talents divided

Given unequally by the master
with hope they will gather interest
An investment in our growth
Though we were scared
for the master is shrewd
We hid our portion away
Gaining nothing
Fearful of His return
since we suspect
we were wicked

Talents buried like seeds
under hard earth
Expected to grow
in a space of no blooming
Tangled in choking weeds
these shallow talents wither
Birds peck at the remains
No roots can find purchase
and any fruit is shriveled and bitter

Talents hidden under bushels
Her light so bright
it made others jealous
They tried to snuff her out
so she would not set
the world aflame
So she could not burn them
Yet her spark remains
It smokes and smoulders
waiting for fuel
to be added to the embers

Talents guarded by magpies
who peck at these glittering jewels
Try to dislodge them
To steal for their own
and woman was the brightest gem of all
Her loveliness drew millions
to gaze at her in wonder
and take credit for how
Their pressure formed her

Talents locked in pine pew boxes
slaves climbed inside
to be smuggled
to a place of freedom
Far from our pain that shackles
From the lie of worthlessness
The loss of them mourned
by we who would possess them
We who forget
how we threw them to the lions
How shocking they survived
How frightening that
they might do unto others
what has been done unto them
That they might use
our own whips against us

Talents barricaded by heavy gates
that will not budge
unless we brace our backs
and push together as one
Forge the key
Force the lock
Nail our manifesto to the door
Make a proclamation
of our desire
to set our precious

Talents Free

The artist got it right
Piecing shards of glass methodically
Sorting the colours
Binding them together
until the picture emerges
One seamless piece
of spectacular beauty
to lift the heart

A lesson lurks in the design
of windows fixed in church buildings
An ideal to aspire to
A church crafted to welcome the downtrodden
A rich life fused with the spectrum of vibrant hue
A home where our edges fit snuggly against one another
to form one magnificent picture

A harmonious composition
crafted with broken glass
A glorious church
constructed from

Broken People

Be the clay
Pliable and captivating
Let the potter mould you
Let the Lord shape your form

So they dipped themselves
in our holy water
Sponged at the salty streams
washing over them
Scalded themselves in the cauldron
Still their solid
Ashen body remains
Unchanged

We brough down
our hammer on them
calling it a sword
We pummel them
again and again

Dirty
Unnatural
Odious
Crooked
Broken
Crude
Possessed
Abomination

Relentless our blows rain down
until they crack
Are unable to stay
intact under our pressure

This is tough love
we spit

If truthful precision
will break you
you are of no use to us
we say
as we toss the pieces
of them in the street

There in the ally
amongst the grit and grime
He meets them
Picks them up
Dusts them off
Turns them over
to reveal the geode inside

A jewel of great worth
A glimmering flash of amethyst
A dazzling vein of gold
mistaken for fools

This treasure was
never intended to be clay
In no way designed for the kiln
Purchased at high price
Refined with gentle care
Set into crowns

The world already
has copious

Jars of Clay

Your words leave me broken

                                        Shattered

                    in

tiny
                                                            pieces

                              on

              the   hard

cold

                    ground

I pick myself up
Put myself back together
Mended with metal
More beautiful in repair

A golden vein runs through
my cracks
making me stronger
More valuable
than before

Never will I break
in the same place again

So I am learning to love
the imperfection of my

Kintsugi Life

Being thrown
into the fire
will either consume or refine

Woman is gold
Supple and worthy
Radiant and lustrous
She is sought in the dirt
Found clinging to stone

Man is a sugar maple tree
producing sweetness in season
then chopped down and dried out
he burns long and hot
These stoked flames
used to test
your mettle

Woman
find your crucible
Let it hold you safe
while the flames lick at every side

When the dross is removed
woman is cast in the form of Asherah
Bought and sold in the market
Held high on the tallest tower
Her moulded form
brings them to their knees to

Worship Her

We love
because we
were loved first
Lavishly

Love broken open
for us
Poured out
upon our dusty feet
weary from walking
past gardens
and city gates
and grocery store lines

In barefoot stumbling
through muddy markets
the fragrant perfume of love
fades
Is lost
as we are lost
Our pockets empty
We look with longing
at the bread
and wine
piled high
we can not afford

Still in our poverty
we are commanded
to generously give love to our neighbour
Even the one
with the white picket fence
The gorgeous green grass
The stepford wife

But our love
must come from someplace
and our feet forget
where it can be found
Lost in uncleanness
Can not recall
the time they were cared for
with precious perfume
poured from alabaster
and hair
humbly soothing
calloused bunions
warts and all

Maybe
before we give love
we must find
the place it is stored
Open cupboards
Ransack pantries
Flip tables
Knock on doors

Finally in meekness
admit to neighbours
We are all out
and might they please
have a jar of love
to lend us
or even just a cup

To Spare

If you say a prayer for me
do not pray for healing
My wounds have made me sensitive
to the plight of the downtrodden

If you say a prayer for me
do not pray for blessings
I have already taken
more than my measure

If you say a prayer for me
do not pray for prosperity
I have been granted
better than I am due

If you say a prayer for me
ask for power
so I can help shoulder
the burden of another

If you say a prayer for me
pray Forgiveness
My wrongs
outnumbered my good

If you say a prayer for me
beg for wisdom
I do not understand
the harm I do

If you say a prayer for me
do so in remembrance
of bread and wine
I hope unites our

Purpose for Prayer

Every time
I hear our song
I am reminded of you
Of your broken strings
that still sing

In twenty more years
I will still hear those notes
and be grateful for the way
you breathed those lyrics into me
and gave me

Harmony

You are not
a waste of space
You are stardust
exploding into a sun

And I am drawn to you
My body spinning
on its axis
Hoping to glimpse

Your Brilliance

The vibrations of Your voice
are the frequency of creation
The pitch and pulse
The waves that caused
dust to settle into its forms
And the stars are aligned
Concentric circles of birth
Particles floating so close to one another
they seem as one
Zephyr fills the space between
flooding us with the light of the stars
we are assembled from

But darkness sucks us in
Stars collapse
The emptiness tangible
Its pull so strong
we spin closer to the brink

What can fill this black hole
when the meteors of our fears collide
and we collapse in on ourselves
Words swirl through our cells
Between the spaces left for breath
Oxygen to feed the refining fire

Though these coals seem
too dead to rekindle
steel love strikes the flint
A spark catches hold
and a new star

Is Born

On the holy night
when You were born
no birth plan was followed
Did she believe
as I once did
that she might die on the birthstool
that she would not survive bringing
Christ into the world
It was not like our trinket Nativities
Her face pale and peaceful
Arms empty
Belly flat
Instead she would have rested
Spent
Flushed from the straining
Sweat soaked
Eyes streaming
with relief that she had lived
That You had lived

On the night You were born
she would have cried out
Abandoned
as You were on that tree
Mother why have you forsaken me
Scorned for her indiscretion
Spoiled
Tainted
Unfaithful
even in her greatest act of faith
If it were any birth but Yours
any child but You
clutched to the chest of a
homeless
unwed mother

we all would have whispered
behind cupped hands
Is she not from Nazareth
Told her to go home
though she no longer had one
A branch cut from her family tree
Pruned from the line of David

On the night You were born
did Joseph remain at her side
cooing words of a Psalm
as comfort to her ears
Though he should not have been permitted
the law would not allow him to be the first
to look at the face of God
That honour would belong
to the midwives
The women that would have helped her
breathe past the pain
Tell her it was time
to push through the agony
and usher You into world

On the night You were born
she was made impure
by the blood of Your deliverance
bringing new life into the world
Naked You came
and she nourished You
Drawing from her breast
the first communion
This was her body broken
This was her milk spilled

On the night You were born
strangers heralded Your birth
Angels sang in a field
too far away for her to hear
Shepherds came
dirty from their flock
Calling magnificent
A scene so far from glorious
The scent of hay and animals and blood
a heady incense
An offering
only pleasing to the Lord

On the night You were born
she became a Holy Mother
and she knew You
more intimately than anyone
before or since
Breathed in the baby soft
smell of Your head
Counted fingers and toes
Pressed her lips to the
unscarred palms of Your hands
Your unblemished side
and dreamt of Your future

On the night You were born
she treasured all these things
and pondered them in her heart
If by ponder
we mean worried
fretful and sleepless
Awakened often each night
by the need of a child
and the fear they would kill You
Because they came
Because they tried
Because they did

Oh Holy Night

It's in my blood
running down my thighs
Soaking through my cloths
Then rushing to my face
Causing me to wear my heart on my sleeve

It's in my blood
drawn out in tubes
Tested to see what is wrong with me
or bagged and tagged
to be released in the veins of another

It's in my blood
That pools in my flesh
A rainbow of hurt for the world to see my pain
A small scarlet bead that sits on my skin
when I can not help but pick my wounds

It's in my blood
That thin anemic fluid
Causing my head to spin
Making me passive
Rocking me to the edge of sleep

It's in my blood
Beating a frantic rhythm
Moving faster and faster
Racing towards the brink
when I think of him

It's in my blood
A metallic taste on my tongue
The flavour fooling me into thinking I am hard
Reminding me that some day
my blood will be too heavy for my heart to move

It's in my blood
that bathes the child inside me
Lending her my breath
Giving her my sweetness
Like a sourdough passing on leaven

It's in my blood
that I see in the shape of her body
The way her face flushes
pink with blood that she too will shed
The same old cycle to continue

In Her Blood

Carving ourselves
from the inside out
Because the spaces
no one can see
dictate the shape
of us
The lay of the fabric
placed over
these hollow lungs
these broken hearts
these lonely bones

Though these forms
are imperfect
Blemished with
gouges and groves
worn in by the weapons
wielded against us
we have not yielded
Rest assured
we are not without
resources
recourses

Our lifeblood
beats strong and
we are unafraid
of shedding tears
For we know
the power of water
to shape stone
to lend us its energy
to wash our wounds
and ultimately create

New Life

How can something
strong as a tree
be swayed so far
without breaking

How can something
unseen as wind
be powerful enough
to bend and shape it

Learn to lean
like a tree
without snapping

Learn to breathe
like the wind
to transform

The World

They taught me
how to hold a grudge
Delicate and fragile
I never dropped it
Never let it go

They taught me
to say not my will
but theirs be done
Though they are not God
They do not have his eyes

They taught me
not to question
Like a sheep among the flock
never wonder
which of them are the wolves

They taught me
how to pray
forgiveness for the ways
they sinned against me
Claiming they know not what they do

They taught me
mercy is a jug of oil
to be sold for a high price
Never poured out wasteful
on feet in need of cleansing

They taught me
peace is not for the poor
Poverty provides joy
in perpetually striving
against their ties that bind

They taught me
meekness as a Psalm
Guilt a simple tune
Shame a catchy melody
stuck fast in my brain

They taught me
sorrow is a score card
Tick off points in my column
and never let anyone
collect more than I do

But I am learning
to seek new teachers
Ones who search for
the lost sheep
the missing coin

This lesson
is a novel mantra
That I have value
That I have worth
and I still
have so much more

To Learn

This is my breath
Stolen in sips
between the fear
Slowly filling me up
one taste at a time
Hoping to fill me
to the brim
with calm
So there will no longer
be any room left for worry
and all my anxieties can be

Displaced

Emotion is not the enemy
A feeling is not evil

Though maybe we are taught
our fear is wrong
because it is a physical revelation
A body flooded
with the need to fight or flee

And a body
Is less valuable
less trustworthy
than a mind
or a soul
So I have been told

Though this still does not
reasonably reconcile
why the people
who claim fear is evil
are the same ones screaming
about their right
to take up arms and

Fight

Disgrace is a sickness
that has spread
to the tenderest parts of us
Those pieces too soft
to resist the nails
driven relentlessly

Your sin is the spike
Your hand wields the weapon

I have been
whipping myself
with those words
these many decades
My back splintered
from bearing my cross
The weight of it
crushing my bruised spirit
Black and blue
from the blows of shame
and the heavy handed
message that

You alone are the cause
of the horrors of the cross

But I was sent
a Simon
to lift from me my burden
and as he walked with me
he whispered
It was for love of us
that God would

Rent the Veil in Two

I have heard it said
it is always darkest
before the dawn

But how can that be
when I feel myself warming
at the approach of

The Sun

Bodies built
of mostly water
sacrifice
small drops
of their own life
when they shed tears
for the sake
of another's suffering

These are

Holy Tears

I did not want
to come at you
with my title
Set in your mind
a preconceived notion
of who I am

Instead I want you
to read my life
in the margins
of my smile
To revel in
the metaphor of me
Discovering my beauty
deep in the folds
I want to surprise you
with the plenty
these covers can hold
and unveil for you
the mystery
one stretched line
at a time
I want to send you
in search of footnotes
To discover all the places
I have been
Then punctuate
my presence
with the language of
my body
and wait for my story
to unveil

My Name

Why would God
call Themselves
by a name that is
only breath

Unless it was
so that Their name
was the thing that
spoke us into being
and to ensure
They would be
an epitaph
on our lips
in our final cry
The crowning exhale
of life

YHWH

These bones
These dry bones
sat stagnant
for want of flesh
They waited
picked and plundered
for the time when
they would be made
to rise up
To dance again

The wind wailed
Through the valley
Lifting up
these brittle bones
Forming dust
into a body
Breathing life
into expired lungs

Though strength
was slow in building
and these joints
creak like forests in the gale
still they climb
with clawing fingers
Moving toward

The Promised Land

The last few years
have brought to the forefront of the Christian world
a term known as deconstruction

It is difficult to have grown up with an understanding
of who Jesus is
of how much God loves us and
wants us to love each other well
then see the broken ways
the church no longer reflects these same values

Yet I have hope

The mass exodus
from the evangelical church
of some of the most faith filled individuals
is not a source of anguish to me
It is a sign of change
Of a sincere reckoning with what it means
to follow the true teachings of Yeshua

If we believe the first shall be last
and we do
then I fear the current church
is in for a very rude awakening
My prayer is that this book
will be an alarm to wake us all up
Hopefully one that sounds more pleasant
than the blaring fear foghorns
many of us grew up with in the 90s

About the Book

First and foremost, thank you to Christin Taylor who reawakened in me the desire to write, who taught me new ways to hone and polish my words and who championed my work when it was still in it's roughest of rough drafts. I have learned so much from her wisdom and have been blessed to call her friend. Thanks also go out to Christin for connecting me with my incredible editor Lindey Priest. Lindsey managed to teach this uneducated writer so much about form, format, voice, structure, consistency and flow through the critiques and suggestions she made on this body of work. Reading her notes was like a crash course in literature and I am grateful for the ways she assisted me in discovering my own, unique voice. Her perspective on some of the delicate subject matter was invaluable in creating pieces that are more impactful, yet sensitive to potential harm.

To my writer's group, thank you for your encouragement, suggestions and recommendations. It has been so affirming to connect with you and to be inspired by your own incredible work. I believe our little group is going big places.

A huge shout out goes to my favourite little corner of the internet where 9 strangers became incredible friends who have kept me grounded and sane during some of the deepest parts of discovering who I am and who I am meant to be. Abby Glaser, Beth Renker, Elliott Hutchinson, Jeannine Eubanks, Jess Ross, Karis Matthews, Linde Boozell and Renee Horsman have seen the deepest (and most frivolous) parts of me and still stick around. Without your humour, love, encouragement and support I don't know what I would have done during the many, many, many months of lockdown. Thanks for always being in my back pocket.

None of this would have been possible without my wonderful husband, Randall. When I asked him what he though about me spending a year at home, writing a novel, he said, "Sure, there is no sense in both of us working jobs we don't like." Thank you for spending so much time doing something you don't like, for the people you do.

Acknowledgement

Rachel Freeman grew up steeped in the church, attended a private Christian school for 8 years, multiple weekly services, church clubs, being actively involved in youth groups, singing in choirs and worship teams, short term missions and Bible college. However, these things she once counted as gain, she now considers loss, for the sake of knowing deeper faith. This does not mean that she no longer finds value in church community. She still attends and is involved in a local faith community that she loves and believes "get it a lot closer to right". She is thankful they have taken their motto "Journey Together" seriously.

She is a poet living in the wilderness of liminal space that she is exploring with writing. She uses poetry as a tool to exhume the truth buried in the bible, to sort through what relics do not hold value and to polish the gems she discovers along the way.

Rachel took her sweet time realizing she was a writer, a poet, and an author. She always loved writing but didn't believe it could be anything more than a passing fancy due to her struggles with dyslexia and self consciousness over poor grammar and spelling. Thank goodness for writing groups and good editors. Now she has had both poetry and flash fiction published and has written a fiction novel she is currently editing.

She lives in Kitchener, Ontario with her incredible husband who has supported her both physically and emotionally as she has followed her dreams. She has two fantastic children who have taught her so much about loving herself and others better. They are the greatest gifts she could have asked for and far more than she deserves.

About the Author